How To Build Good Writing Habits

Presented by Zak Khan

Website:
Zakwrites.wordpress.com

A Quick Word...

I would just like to take a quick moment to congratulate you for downloading this eBook. Initially, the intention of this eBook was to remind myself of how I went about developing a set of skills and habits that make me the writer that I am today but along the way it has helped others, writers like yourself, to meet their goals and writing objectives. During the 4 months since the release of *How To Build Good Writing Habits*, I went on to write 2 more non-fictional books – 30 Ways To Be More Productive In 30 Minutes and 50 Ways To Write Better Blog Posts.

(Update 24/10/2015) – I've now published more than 10 books on Amazon Kindle

The reason for mentioning this is to draw you attention to the fact that I used the principles in this very book to push myself forward and create books that performed much better than this one. In saying that, the techniques and principles in this book are now available to you but whether or not it can make a difference in your life is completely up to you. Be dedicated, open-minded and passionate about writing – it is the best attitude and approach to any task.

Lastly, I am currently creating a brand new book that completely breaks down the process of writing a book in 14 days.

(Update 18/01/2017) - Wow! It's been a couple of years since I've first published this book and I've had so many people reach out to me sharing exactly how this book has helped them find the courage to start writing. I thank each and every one of you who has taken the time to download, read, review and send me messages. It has been nothing short of amazing!

I felt inclined to revise How To Build Good Writing because in the last 2 years, I've changed quite a bit. My writing has evolved and so has my ideas. No longer am I a student but I'm now a qualified lawyer. Woohoo! More importantly, I've fallen inlove with writing and can see myself publishing books and articles for the rest of my life. It hasn't been an easy road though. Mid 2015 I was diagnosed with an illness that affected my ability to function. Walking was a mission- let alone writing. But, I fought through it and I am now in the best shape of my life. Okay, okay, I won't bore you with my dreadful experiences. What I want to share with you is a small piece of advice that I believe could make an impact in your life.

The fear of failure is far worse than failure. Don't let it prevent you from pursuing a dream. Whether it be writing or singing, if you have a passion for it and your heart truly love it, give it a fair chance. People judge, whether we like it or not. So, if they're going to judge you regardless of what you do or don't do, why not take a shot at something meaningful to you?

With that being said, I've added quite a few more chapters to this book. Some of them are practical whereas others are motivational. I hope you like them. Also, what do you think of the cover I designed for this new edition? Rad, isn't it?

Anyway, I wish you luck on your journey and hope you find pure joy in writing as I and many people around the world have.

How To Build Good Writing Habits

Good writing habits are the foundation to a solid writing career. I remember a time when my keyboard skills were far from adequate. To be frank, my index fingers did most of the work, not to mention that a typical 500 word article took years to finish.

Right now, in a single day I typed this entire book without even needing to look at my keyboard. I don't mean to brag –You could do the exact same thing and I'm going to tell you how.

I was capable of writing 2 eBooks in a single week from one simple technique – **PRACTICE!**

> *"For the things we have to learn before we can do them, we learn by doing them."* – Aristotle

Perhaps, modern life has stripped away the true meaning of **hard work**. I am guilty of a similar crime – technology has influenced my life in an enormous way. The manner in which I think, live and act has become very dependent on latest trends. I'm not proud of this habitual change in thinking.

I don't believe great writers like Stephen King, if given the choice, would change the way his career began. Why? Because word for word, his books were created in a less virtual manner.

Let's face it, writers of the past worked much harder to create books, let alone be published. Does that make them better writers than you and I?

Perhaps!

More importantly, it's safe to say they were harder working writers than we are. By technology spoon feeding us so much, we have fallen into a rut and a habit of laziness.

It's not the apocalypse though. We aren't going to fall so far that we land into a pit of doom and never return to modern society ever again. We will not be writing words from the blood that runs from our damaged fingers, no.

Change is a constant. If we explore practical writing habits and implement them immediately, honing a superior set of writing skills will be achievable.

All I ask of you is to please have the resolve of wanting to change and improve – it's the one intrinsic support structure that will always be reliable. If you, without having any expectations partake in the actionable advice offered in this book, you will build good writing habits.

I guarantee it.

I want to discuss a very important feature to change. Have you ever been introduced to the principle of **Invisible Benefits**?

The name itself leaves very little to the imagination but for the sake of understanding it, I will discuss the relevancy and application of this principle.

If I asked you right now to get off your couch or office chair, go outside and start running for 20 minutes, would you do it? I think not. Let's imagine that I'm your inner voice - that very same voice which asks you to go exercise, go write 500 words, go read a book and so forth.

Would you do it? Highly unlikely, that is, in your current state.

As stated by the book 'The Slight Edge' – *"It's easy to exercise but it's easier not to."* You could immediately get off your chair and run for 20 minutes. In fact, in 24hours, you could easily find 20 minutes to exercise but it's easier not to.

Why?

The benefits of exercising are only acquired after a long period of time – that's why. However, though you may not be losing weight right now, if you did go and exercise you would:

- De-stress
- Promote the release of 'Happy Hormones'

- Feel refreshed and energetic
- Burn calories

From consistent exercise: You would improve your tolerance for stress - **long term**. You would increase your fitness level - **long term**. And all that little calories you burnt over time would add up and result in fantastic weight loss - **long term**.

Those secondary benefits mentioned and those long term benefits are usually invisible benefits. It doesn't manifest immediately, it rarely ever does.

Because you're aware of that fact, it's easier not to try at all. It's easier not doing those easy tasks. That's how our brains have become programmed to think. If we were cavemen, that's a completely different ball game. Getting food was not as simple as heading down to your favourite fast food take out joint. You would have to Hunt – not an easy task at all.

But...they did it.

Survival was the most pivotal aspect at that time. So, no matter the obstacles thrown their way, they found the resolve within themselves to hunt and acquire food.

They had not even weighed the long term benefits. Like learning how to track, hunt and discover. Those invisible benefits occurred but if they hadn't tried to hunt at all and just succumbed to starvation, they would have never achieved those invisible benefits that changed their lives. If anything, humans would have ceased to exist.

Unless you want to write as much as you want to live, you won't truly reach levels that aren't even in your thoughts right now.

You would not reach a level of success that you haven't even considered or thought about yet.

So,

Knowing that building good writing habits comes with *some* small immediate benefits, long term benefits and invisible benefits, are you prepared to work and commit yourself to an easy task?

Are you?

Good! Let's move on...

The Psychology of Practice

Stephen king wrote 10 pages everyday – regardless of weekends or any such holiday. It was a habit which was enforced through practice. Imagine if we were capable of writing 10 pages every day for the next month. You could have 2 if not 3 books completed.

At first glance, I thought to myself – *"Impossible! I don't have the time to write 10 pages. I live a busy life."* And that was that. I made my decision without even weighing the possibilities.

First off, if any man has accomplished a certain task – impossibility is shot straight to hell. Then, my mind began to race. I thought of all that I could accomplish, the possible chances of success if I were to write 3 guides a month and it struck me. Right at that moment, it was like a lightning bolt jolted through me – **I did not have a busy life**.

Perhaps at hindsight it was but realistically, I was filling the time gaps in my schedule with 'filler content' - Nothing of actual significance or benefit to my dreams or goals. All of those filler activities were simply aiding my lazy habits and destroying my chances of success.

Think too much of yourself and you'll fear failure.

Research has stated that a high self-esteem promotes happiness but the flip side is the inflation of Ego. That is quite a dangerous road to be heading down as a writer, right? Your Ego could possibly hold you back from changing or developing better writing habits out of fear. Reason being, when self-esteem is used as an intrinsic motivator, the result of your work can affect your emotional well-being.

If you succeed, your ego inevitable inflates but if you fail, your ego sustains damage which can easily knock a writer into a fearful extremely unhappy state. You may begin to question your resolve as a writer, your thoughts become clouded and you miss one very important point – **Practice makes perfect**.

You will undoubtedly experience failure but it's only meant to push your limits. Your ego could be whispering things to you like – *I'm the Best, I don't need to learn anymore, I will never fail,* then failure creeps up to smash your ego.

It may be painful. It may bruise your confidence but it will not destroy you. Your ego can possibly be holding you back from reaching greater heights. It could be preventing you from practicing new and improved habits of writing. Skills that could double your success rate are just waiting to be practiced.

However, a quality that can be increased through practice and which has a positive effect on your capabilities is confidence. Confidence is developed by successfully attempting to meet an obligation or conquering a difficult task. The difference between confidence and ego is that the quality and level of confidence is built and based on practice and such confidence is increased or decreased based on your competence. The more competent you become at something, the more your confidence increases. An ego can fool you into believing that you are the best when it reality there is plenty of room for improvement. But by practicing as much as possible, you become super competent and able to produce some of the best work that will promote your confidence.

Without beating around the bush, the most important way for you to build good writing habits is through PRACTICE!

Discovery And Growth

Freedom. The ability to explore and discover a path that resonates with you as an individual. Everyone is capable of writing and each of us has a tone that matches our unique personalities.

In any form of art, the ability to be free is the greatest gift an artist can have. Over the last 2 years (2015 – 2017), I dipped my feet into many different waters to find a space that felt like home. I didn't want to just write romance novels because it's profitable or popular. I wanted to find a space I could thrive and shine in. And guess what, non-fiction writing was the space that suited me best.

It allowed me to grow and evolve as a writer and a human being. I won't lie when I say that it pains me to see people still publish substandard books on Amazon because it was wrongfully promoted as 'easy money'. This is no way to grow as a writer. I've tried it and the feeling of disappointment isn't worth the few pennies you'll make.

Writing is not easy. Throwing together a 15 page book isn't going to do anything for you as a writer. What you ought to be looking out for is a challenge. In difficulty, people grow.

Just because I didn't want to enter the romance genre doesn't mean I have not attempted to write romance. An entire novel is stored on my computer collecting virtual dust. Not because I'm afraid to publish it but because I choose to walk a path more fulfilling to me.

You have the freedom of choice.

The beautiful thing about writing is that you get second chances. When you mess up, you can revise and edit.

Every night, for just 15 minutes, I update my journal by hand. What I like to do is be as creative as I can. So much so that some of my journal entries may come across as being weird or written by someone else.

That kind of exploration allows me to discover a voice and tone that is unique to me. I guarantee that if you analyse any prolific writer/author, what they share in common is their individuality. One would expect words on a page to be generic, and to an extent it can be, but someone who writes regularly and experiments eventually develops a uniqueness that stands out.

Sure, grammar and punctuation are all rule based elements of writing but that should not stop you from jumping between different tense, voices, narrations and quips.

At the end of the day, your book IS yours! If you feel like it lacks something special, something unique or something identifiable to you, readers are bound to feel the exact same way.

What I particularly like about exploration is the identification of strengths and weakness. I'm not very good with present tense first person stories. It takes me a considerable amount of time to write large chapters are it would when I write in past tense third person. Boom! A weakness and a strength. With that, I can plan myself to focus my attention towards mastering past tense third person stories.

Like I said above, you have a choice. When something makes you feel miserable, move away from it and move towards something else. Don't just quit and walk away. Talent is not a pre-requisite for writing, hard work and understanding is.

And if you're stubborn like me and simply cannot let something get the better of you, than you can spend an hour a day practicing on the type of writing you suck at in hopes of improving and getting better. In time, you will see results. Emulation is a great way to overcome a learning curve. By placing yourself in the shoes of a writer who thrives with a particular style of writing, you can discover patterns and ideas that make it easier.

Simple enough, right?

Give it a try and let me know how it turns out!

An Apple A Day...

I believe that any doubt we had regarding <u>Practice</u> has been cleared and we can move on to the next segment – building good writing habits. Let's just take a second to analyse what makes a habit good.

- It has an invisible benefit – Only after long periods of practice does the benefit present itself (Abundantly, if I may add).
- They are practicable.
- Good habits are sustainable – Write 2 pages every day? (If not 10).
- You feel content – An apple a day...keeps the doctor away.

If a habit meets 3/4 of the requirements above, it qualifies. You're aware of what is an invisible benefit. However, we need to touch base on practicality.

There's no way to write a 50 Thousand word book in a day. If you can find me someone who has done that from scratch, please feel free to let me know and I'll shoot that 'impossibility' in my mind to hell.

For the sake of this book, let's just go with it being impossible.

On that fact alone, knowing that it's impossible to write 50 thousand words in a single day, are you going to make that your goal? Is that the kind of habit you want to practice? Will that benefit you?

I really hope you answer no. Though writing an entire book in a single day of that quantity sounds amazing, it's not a long term viable option. As a practice, it's not sustainable. You'll suffer from an intensive and terrible burnout within that day.

I guarantee that.

However, what if you were to write 1000 words a day? That is most definitely possible. You could write 200 words every hour for 5 hours and you'd meet that quota.

If you practiced this habit for 10 days, you'd write 10 Thousand words in the space of 50 Hours. Do that 4 more times and you'll have written that 50 thousand word book in a month and a half.

Lesson #1: Set a quota of words to write every single day - Start with 500 words a day!

Do you understand now?

Most of the time, those impossible tasks are made possible when you extend the period of time for completion and take small bites at a time.

Do you have a novel you've been working on? I do. I've been writing this fictional fantasy/paranormal book for the last 3 months. Here's the kicker, I haven't gotten past 10 thousand words.

Why?

I was crafting my book as the ideas hit me.

Things were turning out great when I had an idea but I could go days at a time without a proper unique idea and my book remained on my PC collecting virtual dust.

In the 2 weeks I decided to change this entire game plan. I spent an entire day thinking about the plot, the beginning all over again, the body and the end of the book. By night fall, I had notes on exactly how the story would unfold.

In 13 days I wrote 9 thousand words.

From writing 10 thousand words in 3 months to 9 thousand words in 13 days, I'd say that's a magnificent change. That right there is a sustainable and proper way of maintaining a practicable habit.

Lesson 2: Spend *inspired time* Planning.

When inspiration hits, it's like a storm. That feeling is so powerful that you could drop everything you're doing and rush to your nearest device to start writing, right?

Don't do that.

That burst of inspiration is extremely potent but barely sustainable. Usually, you would use it up within a few hours and by the next morning, you're completely unsure of whether or not you will continue.

And...you won't.

So, instead of spending that inspiration on immediately acting, if you were to use it properly for planning and researching your idea, it's likely that when it wears off, you'll have enough planning completed to follow through.

Lesson #3: Break out of a Toxic Writing Routine

On occasion, writers end up building a routine through practice and planning – the kind of routine that simply damages their career and work. Be it plagiarism to generic content creation, regularly relying on second grade content can have a detrimental effect on your mind and reputation.

Instead, take a few days break. Don't write at all, just think.

The idea behind this lesson is to show you that your world will not end. It's actually better for you to slow down writing than put together content that is toxic for your future.

As a writer, you have to plan for the future but write in the present.

Lesson #4: The Writing Process Takes Place Before You Write

What is it that you do before you fingers hit the keyboard? **You think**.

Words are formulated in your mind, so are ideas, concepts, opinions and deductions. On that premise, thinking plays a larger role in writing and those steps before your hands meet the keyboard are also regarded as writing.

How is this pivotal? As a writer, be it fictional or non-fictional, you're always going to be thinking about your work. Sometimes whilst you're cleaning the floors or when you're in the shower singing, an idea may just hit you and suddenly large amounts of possible content enters your mind.

The actual process of turning those ideas and thoughts into words is just the secondary phase of writing.

That time you spend thinking and conceptualizing is even more important. On that note, it's important that you put core focus and attention on thoughts and research.

Research can set you apart from other writers. It can mould you into a writer that creates work which will be appreciated years from now but most importantly, it will train you to always think as a writer.

The Madness of Writing

Occasionally, I meet people who claim that writing is easy. So easy, that they wouldn't 'waste' their time writing. Now, I can't exactly blame them for thinking that. To the untrained and inexperienced, the thought of someone writing 10 pages every day and becoming one of the most acclaimed writers in the world sounds easy.(Weird thought)

It does.

Just open up word pad and type – boom, writing is as easy as pie. I'm here to say IT'S NOT.

To be honest, writing is one of the hardest and most maddening of careers to pursue. Why do you think so many movies depict writers as hobo, shabby and struggling individuals? Because many writers are struggling, shabby hobo's trying to make a mark on the world.

I am that and I'm not afraid to admit it.

If anything, I'm proud of it. When I open up a word document and start writing, I see the world as it's meant to be. My mind escapes the troubling stereotypes, fears of the unknown and madness of the ignorant.

Some nights, I'm red eyed, drooping and staring into my screen typing long articles like a maniac on Prozac. And you know what? I love it! The challenge it poses to me is exciting. The art of turning a blank document into a piece of art or information fuels my happiness. At the end of that long night, I sleep soundly because without a doubt in mind, the feeling of accomplishment puts me to rest.

Writing, as mad as it is, keeps me sane.

I can't fight it, I can't deny it and I cannot live without it. That is why I will succeed. Not because of arrogance, not because I am the best but because I write as much as I want to keep breathing.

It's a part of my being. Writing is a part of my DNA!

Now, the question remains – how committed are you to writing? If you can dedicate yourself to writing as much as you want to breathe, the sky is the limit. You will transcend to greater heights as a writer and reach success that dreams will never reach.

I promise you, at the very least, with such dedication you can turn into the Stephen King of your world and perhaps someday, someone will be writing about you in some book, the exact same way I have written about King in this book.

10 Core Writing Habits

1. Practice Proof Reading and Error Checking

Rookie mistake and I made it. My ego got the better of me and I thought I was the best. With that mind-set, I discarded the chance of messing up and did not even use any error checking tools. Regardless of how confident you feel, instil the habit of getting your work proof read and error checked.

Do you have any plans of publishing someday? Don't even think of hardcover publishing. Let's start with Amazon digital publishing? Do you have any intention of being a featured author on Amazon?

If you do, I suggest a simple and effective technique. After every page of text, quickly do a free error and grammar check online using free tools! I do not claim that these tools are the best or that they could dispel issues that only real life editors can but a standard error check is better than no error check at all, right?

2. Treat Every Sentence with Importance

Having a time restraint can be quite stressful but do not allow this to impact the quality of your writing. Better late than sorry, unless you feel like every sentence has some value, don't submit. Constructing an article built on filler content can be viewed as generic and impact your quality of success.

I noticed one positive attribute to bestsellers. They possess as little filler content as possible. This is not even based on what critics have to say, from a readers stand point, having a fast paced book with elements being relevant as much as possible promotes a good read.

Think of manga titles. It's a form of storytelling and though you may find some filler content/panels, even these fillers are related to the story at hand.

Simply write each sentence with diligence. Getting consumed by the bigger picture can draw your attention away from those minor details but spending that extra time thinking about each sentence adds up.

Well, it will add up to a well-paced, filler free piece of writing to be proud off.

3. Regular Positive Criticism

Is there anyone you can think off that is capable of giving you honest (sometimes harsh) criticism? As a freelance writer, I've had clients who adored and loved my work and then I had clients who were exceptionally rigid and brutal about any mistakes. In no way am I attempting to paint any of them in a negative light, on the contrary, it's criticism of this nature that helps soften the ego and motivates you to work harder.

If your book is in the initial stages of writing, try blasting a few ideas on someone you trust. Gather some advice in regards to you main plot or premise and work your way down to the finer details.

I find that when talking about my work to other writers, whilst discussing it, mind blowing ideas hit me and I'm refreshed with a great sense of optimism to write.

Do this! Sometimes that criticism and opinions from others can spark the most amazing ideas ever.

If anything, the criticism you receive will make you thick skinned for the future. Worrying or fearing negative reception won't hold you back from: writing, releasing and marketing your work in the future. Ultimately, a writer whose name is out there in the world can be regarded as successful as compared to one who is too scared to even submit their work.

Be brave and bold.

4. Research Thoroughly

The best writers are those that acquire thorough knowledge on a topic. Think about it, an expert is capable of firing knowledge regarding a topic at will. That level of knowledge is what readers are drawn to. They find writers that provide knowledge through quality
as ***trustworthy writers***. Spend 30 minutes researching a typical 500 word article. No matter how informed you believe to be, it's always recommended to brush up on the latest trends and information on any chosen topic.

This step seems to make its way all over this book for a reason, it's blessed important.

Aside from the manner in which you write, the content in which you produce is a huge stepping stone for success. Put out the best possible work to the world and the world will give you the best possible opportunities.

Be proud of the work you produce. The best way for a writer to develop and reach some sort of acclaim is by producing the best possible work. Don't ever regard your readers as dumb. They are smart, intelligent and opinionated – those qualities alone put them in a position of power. You may not realize this but when it comes to writing, readers are capable of deciphering which writers put the most work into their books and they are capable of smelling a passionate writer a mile away.

Give you best and they will promote you as such.

5. Write Every Single Day (Very Important)

Practice makes perfect. I will sing that line from rooftops until it's been drilled into your mind. Write every day of your life. It does not have to be 10 pages, as long as you write. You will improve and garner success over time. This habit is the driving stone to every other habit.

Just think about this for a second. I could write a single eBook for Amazon, release it and fail. That could break me as a writer and the chances of me writing again are slim.

However, let's say that I wrote every single day. No matter how much I earned from my writing, the amount of readers I had and the amount of acclaim I received. I could put together an eBook almost every month. Eventually I'd have a bunch of eBooks on Amazon that are doing okay.

What if, just one book became a bestseller? Is it not possible that all my books will be given the attention and reads they deserve?

Yes, Absolutely. This has happened over and over again on Amazon.

Those writers who continuously and consistently wrote even when no one was reading what they said eventually made it big and successful.

Why? Because of one simple characteristic: Practice/Consistency.

6. Read One Book a Week

Knowledge is power! You and I both know this. It's why we invest our lives into writing every day. We know just how powerful words are and that with words alone, we can change the world.

On that premise, read a book a week. That's not too much to ask for, right?

Even if you spent just an hour a night reading, do it. I'll tell you why. You learn from reading. Am I right? And as a writer, the more we read, the more we learn. Not just information but different writing skills and habits. We pick up on those small details other writer's use which makes their work so interesting.

It boils down to how powerful you want to be. With regular doses of knowledge, the words you use change. That's correct? The power in your words magnifies and with such power, you build on your authority as an Author and Writer.

Why do we spend so many years in school? To Learn! Then suddenly, we complete our studies, acquire a degree and just stop learning. Over a decade of learning and we decide to stop. Wasn't that a routine as well? Wouldn't the elimination of reading have some sort of side effect on your state of mind and life?

It would!

This is how important it is for you to read. Challenge your brain, test your capabilities and develop your knowledge base one book at a time. I guarantee, by the end of your first book, you'd have acquired a new sense of achievement and knowledge as a reader AND writer.

7. Connect With Other Writers

I mentioned this before, technology has changed the world. Everything is built on the possibility of a virtual existence. On that note, writing has transcended to the online world which requires the use of laptops, notebooks, desktops and tablets.

Without exaggerating, it can become quite lonely. Staring into a computer screen all day can have some serious effects on moods and feelings.

Trust me, I write for a living and spend at least 9 hours at my Desktop.

I truly encourage connecting with other writers. They understand the hardship and madness we go through as writers.

Except for the understanding, the idea of building a relationship with other writers in the same boat is comforting. I feel less alone as a writer and it encourages me to meet the standards of my fellow better writers.

This is a healthy way of turning a negative into a positive. I believe that if authors were accommodating to each other and truly helped each other to reach new heights, our success as a collective unit would be monumental.

(*On a side note, feel free to contact me if you need to shoot a few ideas around or just want to connect with fellow writers ☺ my email is at the end of this book*)

8. Dedicate and Complete

There will be instances that test you to your limits. You will be tested as a writer and the odds may even be stacked against you but with dedication and completion, everything will turn out just fine.

Nothing happens overnight. Success may not happen overnight but if you were to write every single day, one odd night success will find you.

This much I know.

It's a game of dedication and commitment. As long as you write and finish pieces, it doesn't matter what challenges you face, all your work will add up and bring to you the best form of writers accolades one can ask for.

Make it a priority to finish projects you start. I know how easily inspiration and motivation can make a person jump from idea to idea but I strongly urge you to never scrap any piece of work without proper thought.

Weigh the pros and cons, the amount of time and energy invested in any piece of writing before hitting the recycle bin.

9. Revisions and Editing

My very first eBook was written, edited and published all within 3 days. Problem is, the first online published version had small errors that I missed.

Why?

Well, I was stupid. Something as simple as Checks and Balances were eliminated in my publishing process. It's not entirely my fault, the excitement of the entire process was rather overwhelming and I made those ridiculous mistakes.

However, experience is one of the best ways to learn.

And learn I did!

If a country requires checks and balances to operate, I'm pretty sure we need to on an individual writing level. Every form of creation requires revisions and editing. I suggest, get in the habit of working with drafts.

Don't just write and immediately release. You could make silly mistakes over and over again which will destroy your reputation and credibility as a writer. I know it's exciting and nerve wrecking to publish, so take your time.

Be certain everything is in place. Ensure all small silly errors have been rectified and then proceed to publishing.

Problem solved!

10. Two New Words Every Day

As a writer, your superpower is words. By increasing your word bank, the possible sentence variations increase. This means, you have more words to work with in an attempt to craft the best sentence possible.

I, for one, have a slightly over standard word bank. It's neither average nor inadequate but not spectacular.

To improve my work, to learn more and write better, I downloaded a word a day app onto my phone. Let me just say, it works and it's helpful.

I probably never would have learnt words such as 'Nidus' or 'Sleuth' without making a conscious effort of getting this application. You could get a dictionary and pick a new word every day as long as you actively partake in learning new words.

Trust me when I say, **knowledge is power.**

Establishing Ground Rules

More often than not, sticking to a plan tends to be the toughest adventure any hero is faced with. You, unlike most heroes, ought to establish some ground rules.

What does writing mean to you? Fuels passion or gives you an escape from the world? Does it provide you with a form of expression or a means to an end? Answer these questions and establish the kind of rules that will keep you grounded as a writer.

It will assist you in sticking to deadlines, improving your overall skill and developing as you progress with time and practice.

Essentially, rules can be bent but not broken unless it's for your undying love of writing.

Remember: *Writing is a form of Art driven by skill.*

Be the Writer

I wanted to save the most important lesson for last as this book deserves to conclude in a very practical manner. More often than not, we all want to be something. Be it a painter, a blogger or even a writer.

However, somewhere along the way we got caught in the "Someday" web. It's a very tough place to get out off and with the vicious black widow waiting to pounce, there's no escaping the "Someday" web except for right now.

Have you started writing yet?

Your book – how far in are you? Generally, people have nothing more than the title written down and a rough idea of the plot. There isn't anything wrong with that but question these very same folks about when they plan to write and the answer will always be - **Someday.**

Someday, I will lose weight. Someday, I will be a writer. Someday, I will stop saying someday.

Wake up call – That ~~Someday~~ is **Today.**

In fact, that someday is **right now**. You can be a writer at this very instant. Being a writer does not mean having a book published. That is completely incorrect. The instant you power up that computer, open up word and begin typing – you have become a writer.

End of story.

So, on that note, I want to end this section with a desperate plea to you. Do not wait until someday to become a writer and to accomplish your dreams. Begin at this very second.

Write now, write later, write for an hour, write for many hours, write a line or write 10 pages.

Just simply write.

Writers Essentials

Though it may be the 21st century and almost everyone has some tablet or desktop around the place, I wanted to kick things back for a while and note down the bare minimum a writer requires.

Consider this the Essentials for kick starting your writing career:

1. A Notepad
2. 2 Pens (Black & Blue)
3. 1 Pencil
4. A Keyboard
5. A Computer
6. **Creative Freedom**

The first 3 items are you bare necessities. Who needs a computer when you can write the old fashioned way, right? It's not as though we are using blood to scribble hieroglyphics on cave walls.

The reason I believe the old fashioned method of writing is essential is because of awareness. We have grown so used to typing that it's become second nature. Sometimes, I can be daydreaming about cats at my desk yet be typing an article like a robot.

In short, there's not much intimacy or a sense of a personal touch to a typed document.

Which is why, I encourage you to use a notepad and pen to jot down notes of a particular idea – it could be a synopsis for your book, a mind map based on research, a time line for your chapter at hand or even an outline for an article.

Then you may proceed to using your computer and creating the product you desire and planned out.

This brings me to the last writers essential: **Creative Freedom.**

What does creative freedom mean to you? I define creative freedom as an escape from the chains of reality. Complete freedom and control of the elements to my fantasies, the freedom to express my inner desires and the freedom to be the hero of my stories.

Creative freedom is subjective. You may find freedom in the manner you choose to write, the way in which your story unfolds or simply the act of being able to think freely.

Regardless of how you define creative freedom – don't let it go to waste. Embrace such freedom, let the words you choose signify the meaning you intended for it and let your mind not be dictated and controlled by the pressures of this world.

Chasing Perfection

I've met many different artists over the years and one thing we all share in common is the pursuit of perfection. Unfortunately, perfection is a subjective ideal which varies from person to person.

As a writer, chasing perfection is a good habit. Years from now I may look back and cringe at all the work I've published and the mistakes I've made. Reason being, in chasing perfection I will get better as a writer.

Improvements and developments will occur and though perfection is an unattainable ideal, my quality of writing will improve drastically.

There is however one catch to chasing perfection. It deals with something we spoke about earlier in this book – Fear.

Fear of not being perfect, fear of not being great and fear of failure is side effects of chasing perfection that results in work being unpublished. Do yourself a favour and remember something very important: In chasing perfection, the only way to track your progress is through reception and reviews.

Ensure that you publish your work regardless of whether or not you're chasing perfection. Allow people to weigh the pros and cons of your work, critically analyse and advise you on ways to improve.

Heck, even allow people to praise you when credit is due. These are all contributing factors to a writer who is consistently and continuously challenging himself/herself.

A writer who doesn't allow words to control him will be able to control the words he writes. At the end of the day, you are the master and manipulator of your own destiny. The path you wish to embrace is completely in your control and for that, you need to separate the chase of perfection for the chase of the dream.

The dream is being a writer.

Pyramid Technique

You may have heard of this from time to time but for the sake of learning new habits, let's begin with a brief and effective explanation. Pick up a fictional book you may have lying around and find a newspaper article as well. What are the notable differences in the actual construction?

If you notice, the newspaper article begins with the conclusion followed by the details that resulted in the conclusion. Whereas, the fictional book begins with details and builds up to huge conclusion at the end of the book.

And that is what we call the pyramid technique.

This is actually a very important technique as it can be viewed as the foundation to writing. I want you to think about the audience you desire - the kind of people who would show an interest in your work.

Are they one for mystery or facts?

In other words, are they a fictional or non-fictional group of readers? If you choose fictional – you would follow the pattern of revealing details from the beginning up until the conclusion which will be huge.

If you choose non-fictional – you would follow the pattern of beginning with your findings/conclusion and then introduce your details which back up and give further information to your conclusion.

Nevertheless, when working with fiction, get a large sheet of paper out and in the centre write down the conclusion. Draw a circle around that and attach legs all around the circle. At the end of each leg, fill in a detail of your story. Do this over and over again, circle up important details and create legs amongst those to fill in sub-details to your details.

Soon, you'll have a complete mind-map or spider diagram containing all the pivotal details of your story. Furthermore, scatter and rearrange these details according to the way in which you want to reveal it to your audience, create a time line and insert particular details into particular spots.

I guarantee that at the end of this activity, you will have the time slots and arrangement of your story all on paper.

Use Your Different Senses

It may just be safe to say that as a writer, be it in fiction or non-fiction, your ability of evoking the different senses of your readers through strategic word combinations is what could make you extremely successful.

Think about it for a second.

How amazing is it when reading a book and the writer best describes a steaming fresh bowl of creamy cheesy pasta. With each bite, the freshly spiced pasta leaves you completely fulfilled and satisfied.

I don't about you but I could almost taste it, smell it and sure to hell crave that pasta now.

In saying that, when writing your book or article, embrace the concept physically. Go take a walk in the garden if you plan on writing a particular piece dealing with the outdoors. Breathe the fresh air, feel the tree barks that aged along with you and take a whiff of the scented flowers all around you.

Activate your sense and use that to write. Allow yourself to infuse your physical surroundings and the experience you had with activating your senses and describe it in words.

That, in my opinion, has proven to be the best form of creative writing that triggers the different senses.

A writer that experiments and is capable of making his/her reader experience these senses along with him/her is bound to create a compelling piece of art. Think of it this way, don't just tell the story – Live the story. Let you reader feel like he or she is experiencing everything in real time. Invest some time, energy and thought into senses activation and create spectacular content.

Deconstruct Your Design

I want you to paint a picture in your mind. A motion picture of how you would like to see your story play out. Be it part by part, like in a movie with different scenes. As this occurs, put together the pieces in your mind and construct an overall picture of what you plan to write.

Follow this up by writing down a broad overview of that very same mental picture you drew.

As you go about doing this, imagine you're piecing together a huge puzzle that forms 'Your Story'. Now, once you've accomplished this small feat, deconstruct such picture piece by piece.

Reason being, a story is the construction of chapters or mini scenes. These scenes when put together form the big completed picture. When you deconstruct the design, it enables you to work on the mini pieces, the chapters, individually without losing sight of the overall design.

Remember, this your design.

When fleshing out your chapters, begin by summarising the chapter in essence. It need not be more than a few lines. By doing this, you can start fleshing out the details surrounding the purpose and main plot development of such particular chapter through the summary. This will ensure that you not lose sight of the whole picture whilst creating a mini-picture for each chapter.

The way it looks, manifests, develops and pieces together is completely in your control. Thus, to prevent mishaps whilst preserving the original chosen concept, you may change and edit these chapters as you wish without destroying your design.

Use this technique in sync with The Pyramid Technique. Together, they will ensure that you are organized and capable of crafting a picture that is simply magical. Every formula requires steps and practice.

I've given you the steps - it's your turn to implement and practice.

The Slight Edge Writer

I consider myself a slight edge apprentice. It's a philosophy that I live by and which has helped me achieve significant success and change in my life. Be it from conquering gluten and wheat intolerance, starting a business from scratch, writing an EBook or successfully completing workout programs like Insanity, Insanity the Asylum and so forth.

The most important principle learnt from The Slight Edge is consistently doing the **easy** small tasks every day for a long period of time. I could never do justice to a magnificent book in just a few lines but the above principle in my opinion can make the greatest impact.

As you grow closer to the conclusion of this book, you would have most certainly penned down and understood many of the writing habits mentioned but simply acknowledging these habits is not enough.

It is up to you, as a writer, to implement these simple, easy to do habits every day without expecting a short term fix or miracle. It's easy not to do any of these habits but it's also **easy to do** them.

Neither is it rocket science nor impossible.

The change which you desire as a writer, the success which you desire as a writer, the work which you desire to produce as a writer will only manifest upon the application of these small but potent habits.

How would you describe your attitude?

If I challenged you to unbiasedly profile yourself as a character in a book, how would you describe your attitude? Do you have a burning desire to accomplish that which you dream about or are you plagued by the fear of failure? Are you consumed by happy, optimistic thoughts or is your mind consumed by insecure possibilities?

I want you to profile yourself and if you cannot honestly say that you have a good, healthy and happy attitude – you will have identified a huge set back in your life.

Your outlook on life as a writer weighs heavily upon the work you produce. It could be fuelling your lack of confidence by feeding on your fears and dragging other down alongside you. Be a part of a group who are positive and happy – be one of those happy people as well. Change your outlook on life, acknowledge your small accomplishments and improve your attitude.

The company you are and the company you keep will forever decide the outcome of your actions.

Baby Talk & Conspiracy Theorists

"Mama, how are babies made?"

"Well, love, when mama and papa love each other and want to have a baby, they place an order with the supreme council of babies who then does a special investigation. They take mamas and papas love and magically send us the best baby in the whole wide world. That's you!"

This is sort of a conversation I've watched parents spin to their kids over and over again.

More often than not, kids start asking a bunch of questions about this magical supreme council of babies and the parents come up with more cute and creative replies.

All of a sudden, parents turn into the best storytellers.

Then you have conspiracy theorists who come up with weird and 'out of this world' explanations for events that cannot be explained.

Aliens, supernatural beings, scientific experiments or government cover up, they think of it all.

But guess what, logically, someone may think these explanations are ridiculous but as a writer, those stories can make pretty entertaining reads.

A quick and fun habit I've developed in the last year has been to conjure up weird explanations for anything and everything.

I try to paint different stories for events that happen to me or others, I pull out a newspaper and read crimes with the aim of explaining what happened or piecing together fictitious facts that could reveal who is guilty and why they committed a crime.

All it takes is 15 minutes of your time every day.

It requires nothing from you besides creativity. There's no right or wrong explanation. Be as creative and wild with your imagination as possible. Do that and watch how much easier it becomes to work on plots and creative details for characters.

Use an excuse to come up with reasons for events, be suspicious, ask questions and spin tales that seem ludicrous until they don't. Make a note of those ideas that seem the most entertaining to you and could be used as a good story. Hell, I've even used dreams as the motivating idea to craft an entire story.

Like I said, there's no right or wrong way to be creative.

Showing Up – The Basic Habits Of Writers Who Succeed At Marketing

Sigh, how easy life would be if all you had to was write a book and then it automatically becomes a bestseller!

Sadly enough, that's not how the world works.

Reality requires us writers/authors to be a tad bit multitalented. I've spoken about this in my recent book called **The Productivity Handbook For Lazy People**, wherein I delve into a system of developing core habits and qualities that promote your probability of success.

And I say 'probability' because any writer who dedicates years of his life to the craft, he or she will be successful. But, it all comes down to whether people actually know about you and what you're working on.

In this digital age, blogs, social network accounts, YouTube and websites are all essentials that cannot be ignored.

Rarely do I witness an author publish a book in stores and it magically becomes a success.

Heck, that's rarely ever been the case even before Facebook and blogs blew up. Newspapers and magazines were the go to form of marketing. Wait, even better than that, launch events were hosted all over with an author meeting as many people as possible in hopes of convincing them that what he has worked on is worthy of their time and money.

Competitions never fail to be an effective strategy to gather large amounts of shared attention towards your work. It requires some form of capital input but the results are usually satisfactory when conducted effectively.

Nevertheless, updating people on what you're working on and what your goals are is a splendid way of showing up.

Think about it this way, you have to insert a plug into a socket to send electricity to whatever it is you are trying to use. Similarly, plugging yourself and work into society is a mandatory way of sparking interest and gathering as much eyes to your work as possible.

Write a blog post once a week and connect with your readers.

Loop them in and let them know how important writing is to you. Those individuals who notice you will support you through thick and thin. I've learnt this from personal experience.

You have no idea how many people message me after reading this book to relate how inspired they feel to start writing and motivating me to keep working hard.

I may not be the best right now but I'm working towards it. What I find weird is when people decide to abandon a dream when they realize it may take years to accomplish.

However, 10 years from now you're going to be 10 years older. How about being 10 years older and a bestselling author or a doctor or singer?

The time will pass either way so don't use that as an excuse to quit because it's a poor reason.

I want you to make a habit of posting once a week on a blog or YouTube about your progress as a writer and regularly, at least once a day, tweet or mention something related to writing.

It shouldn't take you more than 30 minutes to write a quick 200 word update on a blog so there's no reason to miss even one blog post.

30 minutes a week can turn into 30 subscribers and 30 readers who work with you to make your book a success.

Your time and effort will not go unnoticed if you just show up.

The Beginning of Your Journey...

I firmly believe that if you apply and practice everything in this guide, you will develop into a magnificent writer. Remember, the most important characteristic of a writer is dedication.

Never succumb to negative reviews, never give up because of failure and don't allow yourself to be controlled by fear.

Get up each day with renewed vigour. Tackle every page with dedication, passion and confidence. Not only will you build good writing habits, you may just create a number #1 bestseller in a number of weeks.

I want to conclude by wishing you all the best in your journey as a writer. Let every experience you encounter be a lesson, challenge yourself every single day and push the boundaries.

In the end, when your day comes to a close, you can proudly say that it's been a day of positive writing.

All the best,

Zak.

To get in contact, hit me up with an email at: TheZakKhan@gmail.com or visit my website: Zakwrites.wordpress.com

Note: *Please be kind enough to leave a review of this book on Amazon or Goodreads, thank you so much.*